D0640809

Managing Editor • Art Worthington

Publishers • Lawrence Siegel & Art Worthington

Cover Design • Peter Hess

Designer • Liz Howard

Writing & Research • Liz Howard

Facilitator • Pamela Thomas

.com

(800) 541-3533

1776 • Across 110th Street • The Adventures of Barry McKenzie •
Cage • Blacula • Bone • Boxcar Bertha • Buck and the Preach
The Carey Treatment • Conquest of the Planet of the Apes • The Co
You Always Wanted to Know About Sex (But Were Afraid to Ask) •
Fritz the Cat • Frogs • The Fury of the Wolfman • The Getaway •
Kid • The Hot Rock • Images • J. W. Coop • Jeremiah Johnson
The King of Marvin Gardens • Lady Caroline Lamb • Lady Sings
in Paris • Left Hand of Gemini • The Legend of Nigger Charley •
Man of La Mancha • Mary, Queen of Scots • My Name Is Shangha
Now You Don't • The Other • Pete 'n' Tillie • Pink Flamingos •
Adventure • Prime Cut • Shaft's Big Score • Skyjacked • S
Sounder • Super Fly • They Only Kill Their Masters • Treasure Isla

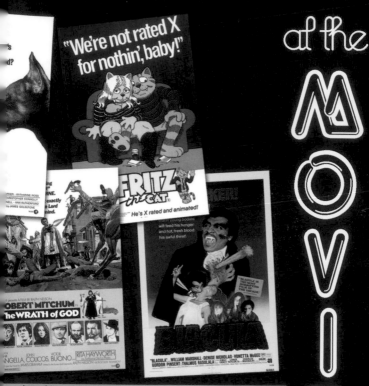

at the

MOVIES

Another Nice Mess • Avanti! • Ben • The Big Bird
• Butterflies Are Free • Cabaret • The Candidate
oys • Deliverance • Dynamite Chicken • Everything
t City • Fillmore • The Final Comedown • Frenzy
e Godfather • Harold and Maude • The Heartbreak
Joe Kidd • Junior Bonner • Kansas City Bomber
Blues • The Last House on the Left • Last Tango
e Life and Times of Judge Roy Bean • Los Amigos
e • Napoleon and Samantha • Now You See Him,
y It Again, Sam • Pocket Money • The Poseidon
hterhouse-Five • Sleuth • Snoopy Come Home
• What's Up, Doc? • The Wrath of God

TOP GROSSING FILMS OF 1972

1. The Godfather $86,691,000
2. The Poseidon Adventure $42,000,000
3. Cabaret $28,000,000
4. Deliverance $22,600,000
5. What's Up, Doc? $21,900,000
6. Jeremiah Johnson $20,250,000
7. The Getaway $18,000,000
8. Lady Sings the Blues $9,665,000
9. Everything You Always Wanted to Know
   About Sex* (*But Were Afraid to Ask). $8,828,000
10. Sounder $8,726,000

Oscars® Presented in 1972
for 1971 films

Best Picture
THE FRENCH CONNECTION

Best Actor
GENE HACKMAN,
THE FRENCH CONNECTION

Best Actress
JANE FONDA, KLUTE

Best Director
William Friedkin,
THE FRENCH CONNECTION

Best Supporting Actor
BEN JOHNSON, THE LAST PICTURE SHOW

Best Supporting Actress
CLORIS LEACHMAN,
THE LAST PICTURE SHOW

Best Song
"THEME FROM SHAFT,"
SHAFT

Oscars® Presented in 1973
for 1972 films

Best Picture
THE GODFATHER

Best Actor
MARLON BRANDO,
THE GODFATHER

Best Actress
LIZA MINNELLI, CABARET

Best Director
BOB FOSSE, CABARET

Best Supporting Actor
JOEL GREY, CABARET

Best Supporting Actress
EILEEN HECKART,
BUTTERFLIES ARE FREE

Best Song
"THE MORNING AFTER,"
THE POSEIDON ADVENTURE

THE ACADEMY AWARDS

PRIMETIME LINEUP

		7:00	7:30	8:00	8:30	9:00	9:30	10:00	10:30
SUNDAY	ABC	Local	Local	The F.B.I.			ABC Sunday Night Movie		
	CBS	Local	Anna and the King	M*A*S*H	Sandy Duncan Show	New Dick Van Dyke Show	Mannix		
	NBC	Local	The Wonderful World of Disney		NBC Sunday Mystery Movie: Columbo/ McCloud/McMillian and Wife/Hec Ramsey			Night Gallery	
MONDAY	ABC	Local	Local	The Rookies		ABC Monday Night Football			
	CBS	Local	Local	Gunsmoke		Here's Lucy	Doris Day Show	New Bill Cosby Show	
	NBC	Local	Local	Rowan & Martin's Laugh-In		NBC Monday Night Movie			
TUESDAY	ABC	Local	Local	Temperatures Rising	Tuesday Movie of the Week			Marcus Welby, M.D.	
	CBS	Local	Local	Maude	Hawaii 5-0		CBS Tuesday Night Movie		
	NBC	Local	Local	Bonanza		The Bold Ones: The New Doctors		NBC Reports	
WEDNESDAY	ABC	Local	Local	Paul Lynde Show	Wednesday Movie of the Week			Julie Andrews Hour	
	CBS	Local	Local	Carol Burnett Show		Medical Center		Cannon	
	NBC	Local	Local	Adam 12	NBC Mystery Movie: Madigan/ Cool Million/Banacek			Search	
THURSDAY	ABC	Local	Local	Mod Squad		The Men: Assignment Vienna/ Delphi Bureau/Jigsaw		Owen Marshall	
	CBS	Local	Local	The Waltons		CBS Thursday Night Movie			
	NBC	Local	Local	Flip Wilson Show		Ironside		Dean Martin Show	
FRIDAY	ABC	Local	Local	Brady Bunch	Partridge Family	Room 222	Odd Couple	Love, American Style	
	CBS	Local	Local	Sonny & Cher Comedy Hour		CBS Friday Night Movie			
	NBC	Local	Local	Sanford & Son	Little People	Ghost Story		Banyon	
SATURDAY	ABC	Local	Local	Alias Smith & Jones		Streets of San Francisco		The Sixth Sense	
	CBS	Local	Local	All in the Family	Bridget Loves Bernie	Mary Tyler Moore Show	Bob Newhart Show	Mission: Impossible	
	NBC	Local	Local	Emergency		NBC Saturday Night Movie			

television

The Waltons

The Rookies

Maude

The Bob Newhart Show

The Sandy Duncan Show

The Streets of San Francisco

Sanford and Son

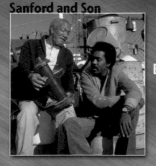

new shows

Emergency!

Bridget Loves Bernie

Fat Albert and the Cosby Kids

The Brian Keith Show

Kung Fu

M*A*S*H

Schoolhouse Rock!

Shouldn't malt liquor be called malt beer?

Not this one.

This is BUDWEISER Malt Liquor.
It's America's only 100%-malt, malt liquor
(no other grains added).
That makes it the first malt liquor that
really is...malt liquor.

The first malt liquor good enough to be called BUDWEISER.

ANHEUSER-BUSCH, INC. ST. LOUIS

1. All in the Family

3. Marcus Welby, M.D.
4. Gunsmoke
5. The ABC Movie of the Week
6. Sanford & Son
7. Mannix
8. Funny Face

2. The Flip Wilson Show

9. Adam 12

top 20 shows
october '71 - april '72

10. The Mary Tyler Moore Show

16. The Partridge Family

11. Here's Lucy
12. Hawaii Five-O
13. Medical Center
14. The NBC Mystery Movie
15. Ironside

17. The F.B.I.
18. The New Dick Van Dyke Show
19. The Wonderful World of Disney
20. Bonanza

The less you spend on a car, the more you can spend on other things.

This car gets up to 40 miles to the gallon.

Up to 75 miles an hour.

Overhead cam engine, rack and pinion steering, 4-speed synchromesh transmission, power-assisted front disc brakes, front bucket seats, radial tires, tachometer, racing mirror. All standard equipment.

Oh, it doesn't have automatic transmission, air conditioning, and a 400-horsepower engine.

But which would you rather have? Automatic transmission, air conditioning, and a 400-horsepower engine?

Or Michelle and Tammy and Alison?

The Honda Coupe. Under $1700.
It makes a lot of sense.

ON THE RADIO

10538 Overture - Electric Light Orchestra; A Horse with No Name - America; Alone Again (Naturally) - Gilbert O'Sullivan; America - Simon & Garfunkel; American Pie - Don McLean; Anticipation - Carly Simon; Baby, Don't Get Hooked on Me - Mac Davis; Bang a Gong - T. Rex; Ben - Michael Jackson; Best Thing - Styx; Black and White - Three Dog Night; Black Dog- Led Zeppelin; Brandy (You're a Fine Girl) - Looking Glass; Burning Love - Elvis Presley; The Candy Man - Sammy Davis, Jr.; The Cisco Kid - War; The City of New Orleans - Arlo Guthrie; Conquistador - Procol Harum; The Cover of the Rolling Stone - Dr. Hook & The Medicine Show; Crocodile Rock - Elton John; Day After Day - Badfinger; Day by Day - Godspell; Day Dreaming - Aretha Franklin; Diary - Bread; Doctor My Eyes - Jackson Browne; Do It Again - Steely Dan; Don't Let Me Be Lonely Tonight - James Taylor; Everything I Own - Bread; Family Affair - Sly & the Family Stone; The Family of Man - Three Dog Night; The First Time Ever I Saw Your Face - Roberta Flack; Garden Party - Rick Nelson; Goodbye to Love - The Carpenters; Heart of Gold - Neil Young; Hold Your Head Up - Argent; Honky Cat - Elton John; I Am Woman - Helen Reddy; I Can See Clearly Now - Johnny Nash; I Need You - America; I Saw the Light - Todd Rundgren; I'd Like to Teach the World to Sing - The New Seekers; I'd Love You to Want Me - Lobo; (If Loving You Is Wrong) I Don't Want to Be Right - Luther Ingram; I'll Be Around - The Spinners; I'll Take You There - The Staple Singers; Isn't Life Strange - The Moody Blues; It Never Rains in Southern California - Albert Hammond; Jesus Is Just Alright - The Doobie Brothers; Join Together - The Who; Layla - Derek and the Dominos; Lean on Me - Bill Withers; Legend in Your Own Time - Carly Simon; The Lion Sleeps Tonight - Robert John; Listen to the Music - The Doobie Brothers; Long Cool Woman (In a Black Dress) - The Hollies; Me and Julio Down by the Schoolyard - Paul Simon; Me and Mrs. Jones - Billy Paul; Mother and Child Reunion - Paul Simon; My Ding-a-Ling - Chuck Berry; Old Man - Neil Young; Operator - Jim Croce; Papa Was a Rollin' Stone - The Temptations; Puppy Love - Donny Osmond; Rocket Man - Elton John; Rockin' Pneumonia and the Boogie Woogie Flu - Johnny Rivers; Rockin' Robin - Michael Jackson; Roundabout - Yes; Saturday in the Park - Chicago; School's Out - Alice Cooper; Song Sung Blue - Neil Diamond; Summer Breeze - Seals and Crofts; Superstition - Stevie Wonder; Take It Easy - Eagles; Taxi - Harry Chapin; Tiny Dancer - Elton John; Too Late to Turn Back Now - Cornelius Brothers & Sister Rose; Ventura Highway - America; Walkin' in the Rain with the One I Love - Love Unlimited; Where Is the Love? - Roberta Flack & Donny Hathaway; Witchy Woman - Eagles; You Don't Mess Around with Jim - Jim Croce; You Wear It Well - Rod Stewart; Your Mama Don't Dance - Loggins and Messina; You're So Vain - Carly Simon

Music

Pink Floyd debuts their album Dark Side of the Moon *in January which they play in its entirety at a concert in England. The album will not be released for another year.*

The Eagles release their first album, The Eagles, *which includes the hits* Take It Easy, Witchy Woman *and* Peaceful Easy Feeling.

Don McLean's hit, American Pie, *is at the top of the charts in America, England, Canada, France, Australia, Poland, Germany, Holland and Norway. The song contains the phrase "The day the music died"—which refers to the day that Buddy Holly, Ritchie Valens and J. P. "The Big Bopper" Richardson were killed in a small plane crash—is incredibly popular and will eventually be listed as the number five song on the Songs of the Century list, a compilation of 365 songs of historical significance in the 20th century.*

The band America re-releases their 1972 self-titled debut album early this year; this time it includes the song A Horse with No Name and the album is #1 on the U.S. album charts for five weeks. Their second album, Homecoming, *is released in November which peaks at #9 on the album charts.*

Notes

Blue Öyster Cult releases their self-titled debut album.

The Partridge Family's teen heartthrob, David Cassidy, releases his first solo album, Cherish.

Jackson Browne releases his self-titled debut album.

Grateful Dead's guitarist, Jerry Garcia, releases his first solo album, Garcia.

Lou Reed, the guitarist, vocalist and song-writer of the recently defunct band The Velvet Underground, releases his first solo album, Lou Reed as well as his second solo album, Transformer, this year.

Mardi Gras, the last studio album by Creedence Clearwater Revival. is released before the band breaks-up this year.

LOS ANGELES, CALIFORNIA

1972 Advertisement

New Ford Ranchero...
Right on!

AM/FM Stereo Radio—with space-age microcircuitry, surrounds you in faithful stereo sound.

Hood Scoop Standard on GT Model—furnished with Ram-Air induction on 351 (4V) and 429 V-8 engines.

Super Wide G-70s—really grab the road when you want to hang in there.

High-back Bucket Seats—for individual comfort; high-back bench seat is standard.

Deluxe Three-spoke Steering Wheel. Rim-blow feature gives fingertip horn control.

Performance Cluster—includes tachometer, odometer, clock, ammeter, water temperature and oil pressure gauges.

Four-on-the-floor—fully synchronized 4-speed transmission with quick-shift Hurst® mechanism.

Magnum 500 Chrome Wheels—the ultimate in "mag" type wheels. Available on all models.

No question of who you are in a Ranchero, because your Ranchero can be a one-of-a-kind pickup, designed by you from a string of with-it options you wouldn't believe. Some are shown above. And

Ranchero's all new for '72. New size, new style, new engineering, new satisfaction. And the pickup box is both wider and longer. Visit your Ford Dealer and check the specs. Then roll your own!

A better idea for safety: Buckle up.

FORD RANCHERO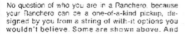

AWARDS

GRAMMY AWARDS

RECORD OF THE YEAR:
The First Time Ever I Saw Your Face
Roberta Flack

ALBUM OF THE YEAR:
The Concert for Bangla Desh
George Harrison, Ravi Shankar, Bob Dylan, Leon Russell, Ringo Starr, Billy Preston, Eric Clapton and Klaus Voormann

SONG OF THE YEAR:
The First Time Ever I Saw Your Face
Ewan MacColl, writer

BEST NEW ARTIST:
America

BEST POP VOCAL, MALE:
Without You
Harry Nilsson

FEMALE:
I Am Woman
Helen Reddy

DUO, GROUP/CHORUS
Where Is the Love
Roberta Flack and Donny Hathaway

The NOBEL PRIZE IN LITERATURE
is presented to
Heinrich Böll
Federal Republic of Germany

"for his writing which through its combination of a broad perspective on his time and a sensitive skill in characterization has contributed to a renewal of German literature"

PULITZER PRIZES

PUBLIC SERVICE:
The New York Times
For the publication of the Pentagon Papers.

POETRY:
James Wright
Collected Poems

HISTORY
Carl N. Degler
Neither Black Nor White

BIOGRAPHY OR AUTOBIOGRAPHY:
Joseph P. Lash
Eleanor and Franklin

MUSIC:
Jacob Druckman
Windows

DISASTERS

WEST VIRGINIA: Just four days after being deemed satisfactory by a federal mine inspector, a coal slurry dam above Buffalo Creek Hollow, bursts, releasing some 12 million gallons of black sludge. A 30-foot-high wall of black water races down Buffalo Creek, burying 16 hamlets with a combined population of 5,000. 125 are killed, 1,121 injured, and more than 4,000 left homeless.

FARS: A strong earthquake rips through the Fars province south of Iran. The 7.0 quake kills nearly a quarter of the 23,000 residents within a 30-mile radius of the epicenter.

IDAHO: 91 men die in a silver mine in Kellogg when an underground fire sends smoke and carbon monoxide pouring through the tunnels.

SOUTH DAKOTA: In the Black Hills the Canyon Lake Dam fails when the water level rises 12 feet in under 2 hours. 15 inches of rain falls

in 6 hours causing creeks in the area to overflow their banks, including Rapid Creek, which flows through downtown Rapid City. The dam breaks, sending additional water into the already swollen Rapid Creek, and it begins to flow at more than 10,000 cubic feet per second. The floodwaters barrel through Rapid City at 12:15 am on June 10th, resulting in 238 deaths, 3,057 injuries, and more than $160 million in damage.

SOUTH AMERICA: A plane carrying 45 passengers, most of them members of a rugby team, crashes in the Andes mountains on October 13th. 29 passengers survive the crash and part of the fuselage remains intact providing some shelter from the harsh elements. In the days following the crash

some of the survivors succumb to the extremely cold conditions at 14,000 feet and eight are killed in an avalanche that sweeps over the shelter. Faced with no food, no heat and radio reports that the search had been called off, the survivors resort to cannibalism. Ultimately 16 are rescued on December 20th, after two of the survivors make a 12-day hike over the Andes and find help.

In Nicaragua's capital city, Managua, 5,000-12,000 people are killed by a 6.25 earthquake. Foreign aid pours in to help the victims but little reaches them, and eventually Nicaragua's President Somoza is accused of pocketing millions of dollars of relief money.

CALIFORNIA: A restored F-86 Sabrejet that had been on display at an air show in Sacramento fails to become airborne during takeoff from Sacramento Executive Airport. The jet skids off the end of the runway,

exploding in a ball of flames when it crashes into a Farrell's Ice Cream Parlor. 12 children and 10 adults die and another 38 are injured. Amazingly the pilot survives the crash with just a broken arm and cuts on his face. Sadly, pilot error is eventually determined to be the cause of the crash, as the nose of the craft was prematurely raised, resulting in excessive drag and a partially stalled condition.

EAST BERLIN: An Ilyushin airliner crashes, killing all 156 people on board.

81 Survive Plane Crash;
Death Toll Jumps to 96

U.S. Team
Probes
Cause

FLORIDA: On a moonless night in late December, Eastern Airlines Flight 401, a new Lockheed L-1001 Tristar "Whisperliner" traveling from New York to Florida, experiences what the flight crew believes to be landing gear trouble upon landing approach. The pilots abort the landing, climb to 2,000 feet, and engage the auto-pilot above the Everglades while they try to determine if they have an actual problem with the landing gear or if it is something as simple as a burnt-out bulb on the indicator light. Somehow the auto-pilot is accidently disengaged and the plane begins slowly losing altitude. Over the pitch-black Everglades the descent is so gradual that no one notices the altitude loss as the cockpit crew continues to struggle with the problem. A visual inspection of the landing gear is underway when the pilot radios the control tower he's ready to begin his second approach. Just seconds later the crew becomes aware they are no longer at 2,000 feet but in fact just above sea level; and a mere 8 minutes after aborting their original landing, the plane's left wing slams into the swampy ground at 227 miles per hour. The wreckage is spread over a third of a mile, bodies and survivors covered in jet fuel and muck throughout the swamp. Of the 176 people on board, 103 die due to injuries sustained in the crash. The landing gear is found to be in the down and locked position and the culprit is two burnt-out lightbulbs.

Agnes, a rare June hurricane and the first of the 1972 Atlantic season, makes landfall on June 19th along the Florida Panhandle causing relatively minor damage. Classified as a Category 1 hurricane, it causes much more damage as a tropical storm making its way across Georgia, the Carolinas, out to sea and landfall again in New York on the 22nd. When it merges with a non-tropical low the following day, the combined system wreaks havoc on the northeastern U.S. until the 25th, causing $2.1 billion in damage over 12 states and 122 deaths. Agnes becomes the first Category 1 hurricane to be retired.

LONDON: A Trident 1 jet crashes two minutes after takeoff from Heathrow Airport and 118 people die.

**Every day
a new success
in adidas** Great victories,
sensational times,
athletic triumphs –
adidas is always there.

For every sport,
for every foot the right shoe –
this is the goal Adi Dassler
has been striving towards
for many years,
thus making adidas the most
successful shoe of all times.

adidas

CRIME IN THE HEADLINES

Samuel Nalo and Robert Comfort are the masterminds behind the Pierre Hotel heist in New York City, which will go down in history as one of the most successful hotel robberies of all time. Along with six other men, in the wee hours of the morning of January 2nd they manage to take hostage of the hotel's skeleton staff of 19. Forcing an employee to hand over the list matching hotel guests to their safe deposit boxes, they proceed to break into the boxes of people whose names they recognize and get away with at least $4 million in jewelry and cash. The burglars are reported to be quite polite and respectful of their hostages and even present each with $20 for their inconvenience before leaving with the loot!

● ● ●

After years of increasingly violent hijackings aboard American airplanes, the FAA issues an emergency rule requiring mandatory inspection of all carry-on baggage and the scanning of all passengers starting in 1973.

● ● ●

All of California's death row inmates have their sentences commuted to life in prison when the California Supreme Court overturns the state's death penalty statute in February.

For eight days in February, U.S. President Richard M. Nixon makes an historical visit to the People's Republic of China, meeting with Mao Zedong.

The Democratic National Committee offices are burglarized and five White House operatives are arrested for the crime on June 17th. On the 23rd President Nixon and White House Chief of Staff H. R. Haldeman are taped while discussing using the CIA to obstruct the FBI's investigation. The tape provides evidence that Nixon has entered into a criminal conspiracy to commit obstruction of justice which is an impeachable offense. In 1974 this tape will prove to be the "smoking gun" of the Watergate investigation, forcing Nixon to resign the presidency rather than be impeached.

Congress votes to send the proposed Equal Rights Amendment to the states for ratification.

The U.S. Libertarian Party holds its first national convention.

After 27 years of military occupation by the U.S., Okinawa is returned to Japanese control.

The IRS and the Bureau of Alcohol, Tobacco and Firearms become two separate entities.

PRESIDENTIAL RACE
The first African American congresswoman, Shirley Chisholm, announces her candidacy for president.

President Richard Nixon and Vice President Spiro Agnew are nominated for a second term at the Republican National Convention.

When the Democratic National Convention meets, Senator George McGovern is nominated for president, and he names fellow Senator Thomas Eagleton as his running mate.

When election day rolls around an apathetic turnout, with only 55 percent of the electorate voting, it ends with Republican incumbent President Richard Nixon defeating Democrat George McGovern in a landslide victory.

WORLD

AUSTRALIA: The Aboriginal Tent Embassy is created outside the Old Parliament House in Canberra, Australia in January when a group of four Aborigines led by Michael Anderson place a sun umbrella on the lawn. In the following days more tents are erected and in February a list of demands for Aboriginal land and mining rights, preservation of Aboriginal sacred sites, and compensation for land deemed not returnable is given to the Australian Parliament. All the demands are rejected by Parliament and in July, Australian police forcibly remove the Aborigines and tents from the area.

BURUNDI: The genocide of the Hutus begins in May when ordered by President Michel Micombero. An estimated 100,000 Hutu people are killed at the hands of the Tutsi Army.

DENMARK: King Frederick IX dies and is succeeded by his daughter, Queen Margaret II.

GHANA: In a military coup on January 13th the prime minister of Ghana, Kofi Abrefa Busia, is overthrown.

GLOBAL: The U.S., the Soviet Union and some 70 other nations sign the Biological Weapons Convention, which is an agreement to ban biological warfare. In Moscow, U.S. President Richard Nixon and Soviet leader Leonid Brezhnev sign the SALT I treaty along with the Anti-Ballistic Missile Treaty and other agreements.

MINERVA: An attempt to form a new sovereign nation, the Republic of Minerva, is made on an artificial island on the Minerva Reefs in the Pacific Ocean south of Fiji and Tonga. Sand is brought in from Australia on barges to form the island in 1972. The nation's founder, Lithuanian-born Las Vegas real estate magnet and political activist Michael Oliver, issues a declaration of independence on January 19th by sending letters to neighboring countries. The Republic of Minerva goes as far as creating their own currency and has lofty goals of creating a libertarian society with "no taxation, welfare, subsidies, or any form of economic interventionism." With little resistance from the new nation, Tonga proclaims the Minerva Reefs as part of their kingdom and the Republic of Minerva collapses.

PHILIPPINES: The entire country is placed under martial law by President Ferdinand Marcos when he issues Proclamation No. 1081.

SRI LANKA: The nation that was formerly Ceylon becomes the Republic of Sri Lanka under Prime Minister Sirimavo Bandaranaike.

TURKEY: The 35th government is formed by Ferit Melen.

UGANDA: President Idi Amin gives Asians living in Uganda 90 days to leave the country, claiming that in a dream God told him to expel them.

VIETNA

M WAR

JANUARY:

- U.S. President Nixon announces an eight-point peace plan for Vietnam and also that Secretary of State Henry Kissinger has been secretly negotiating with the North Vietnamese. The peace plan is rejected by Hanoi.

MARCH:

- The Easter Offensive, a conventional ground campaign, is launched on Good Friday by North Vietnamese forces when they storm across Demilitarized Zone into South Vietnam. NVA's immediate strategy is to capture Quang Tri in the northern part of South Vietnam, Kontum in the mid section, and An Loc in the south. The offensive lasts until October with both sides sustaining heavy casualties.

- The U.S. boycotts the Paris peace talks and Nixon accuses Hanoi of not negotiating seriously.

- The 101st Airborne Division is withdrawn.

APRIL:

- U.S. 7th Fleet targets NVA troops around the DMZ.

- Nixon authorizes a massive bombing campaign of all invading NVA troops, B-52 strikes, and the bombing of Hanoi and Hai Phong harbor.

- The Paris peace talks resume.

- U.S. troop levels drop to 69,000.

MAY:

- NVA troops succeed in capturing Quang Tri City.

- Paris peace talks are suspended indefinitely.

- 125 U.S. military airplanes are ordered into Vietnam.

- Nixon orders Haiphong Harbor and other North Vietnamese ports to be mined and also begins a systematic aerial assault on NVA transportation, oil facilities, and air defense systems.

- South Vietnamese pilots conducting an air strike accidently drop napalm bombs on their own civilians, including children, and the horrific scene of a badly burned young girl fleeing is captured on film.

- The U.S. Army headquarters in Vietnam is decommissioned.

JUNE:

- Aided by the U.S., South Vietnamese troops begin a counter-offensive to retake Quang Tri City.

JULY:

- Paris peace talks resume.

- American actress Jane Fonda visits North Vietnam. While there, she broadcasts antiwar messages on Hanoi radio, is photographed sitting on a North Vietnamese anti-aircraft gun, and visits American prisoners of war (POWs), bringing back messages from them to their families. Later, when reports of torture emerge from returning POWs, Fonda states the former POWs are "hypocrites and liars," and that "these were not men who had been tortured. These were not men who had been starved. These were not men who had been brainwashed." Her actions and words gain her the nickname "Hanoi Jane," and although many years later she apologizes for the photographs, she is still viewed by many Vietnam veterans and their families as a traitor.

AUGUST:

- Kissinger secretly meets with North Vietnamese diplomat Le Duc Tho in Paris again.

- The last U.S. ground troops depart Vietnam.

SEPTEMBER:

- South Vietnamese troops recapture Quang Tri City.

OCTOBER:

- The long stalemate between Kissinger and Tho comes to an end as both sides agree to major concessions. Kissinger, wanting to end the war before the U.S. presidential election in November, even agrees to allow North Vietnamese troops already in South Vietnam to remain there.

- Kissinger visits Saigon and meets with South Vietnam President Nguyên Văn Thiêu to discuss the agreement. Thiêu rejects the agreement, and even when Nixon threatens to cut off all American aid he refuses to accept the terms of the agreement.

- When Thiêu openly denounces the proposal, Hanoi responds by revealing the

VIETNAM WAR

terms of the agreement and then accuses the U.S. of trying to sabotage it.

- On his return to the States a week before the presidential elections, Kissinger states that "peace is at hand," effectively ending any chance George McGovern may have had of winning the election.

NOVEMBER:

- As part of its Vietnamization plan, the U.S. Army turns over the Long Binh military base to South Vietnam.

- U.S. troop levels are down to 27,000 and White House Press Secretary Ron Ziegler states that there will be no further announcements concerning U.S. troop withdrawals from Vietnam. Army advisors and administrators remain to assist South Vietnamese military.

DECEMBER:

- Australian troops are withdrawn following their newly elected prime minister Edward Whitlam's first action using his executive power.

- Secret peace talks between Kissinger and Tho resume in Paris but quickly break down when Kissinger presents a list of 69 changes that South Vietnam President Thiêu wants made to the agreement.

- To force negotiations to resume, Nixon orders the "Christmas Bombings" to begin on December 18th. Eleven days and nights of maximum force bombing of Hanoi draw criticism from the American public, politicians, and media, as well as leaders of other countries and the Pope.

- Swedish Prime Minister Olof Palme compares the American bombing of Hanoi to the Nazi massacres, and as a result of his comments the U.S. breaks diplomatic contact with Sweden.

- North Vietnam agrees to return to negotiations and on the 29th the bombings are halted. Fifteen U.S. B-52s have been shot down and more than 100,000 bombs have been dropped on Hanoi and Hai Phong in this the most intensive bombing effort of the entire war.

1972 Advertisement

IT TAKES SOMETHING PRETTY STRONG TO MAKE PEOPLE TRADE IN THEIR VOLKSWAGENS.

When you buy a Gremlin, you get more than a great little economy car that's fun to drive.

You get a car that's been road-tested and checked over so thoroughly, we make this promise: If anything goes wrong and it's our fault, we'll fix it. Free.

And, if we have to keep your car overnight to fix it, over 1900

AMERICAN MOTORS
BUYER PROTECTION PLAN

dealers will loan you a car. Free.

Finally, you get a name and toll-free number to call in Detroit if you have a problem. And you'll get action, not a runaround.

Nobody in the business does all this for you after you buy a car.

Which is probably why people who've never bought a car from us before are buying one now.

In January, at the end of a peaceful Northern Ireland Civil Rights Association rally in Derry, rioting breaks out in the crowd. British paratroopers, believing they were under attack by armed IRA members, open fire into the crowd, shooting 27 people, 14 of whom are killed. None of the protesters who were shot were armed and five had been shot in the back. The event, which becomes known as Bloody Sunday, steps up the Provisional IRA's campaign of violence against British forces. This year the PIRA kills 100 soldiers, wounds 500, and carries out some 1,300 bombings against commercial targets. In July, as part of their bombing campaign, 22 bombs are set off in Belfast. The event, known as Bloody Friday, kills 9 civilians and 2 soldiers, and leaves 130 injured. The British government responds to the new level of attacks by introducing Direct Rule, ruling Ireland directly from London, as a short-term solution until self-government can be restored to Ireland. Close to 500 people, over half of them civilians, will die in The Troubles this year, the greatest loss of life in any year thus far.

TERROR IN MUNICH

Eight members of a Palestinian militant group with ties to Yasser Arafat, Black September, take members of the Israeli Olympic team hostage in the early morning hours of September 5th in Munich, Germany during the Summer Olympics. Two of the 11 team members are killed almost immediately, the other 9 are held hostage as the terrorists make demands for the release and safe passage to Egypt of Palestinians, non-Arabs and two German radicals jailed in Israel. The Israeli government refuses to comply, and the German government steps in, offering the kidnappers an unlimited amount of money to let the victims go, to no avail. Twelve hours after the first hostage was shot, the Olympic Games are halted. At 10:00 in the evening the kidnappers and hostages are transported by bus to two military helicopters, which take them to a nearby airfield where they are to board a plane taking them to Cairo. Waiting at the airfield are a group of largely unqualified German police who attempt to assassinate the kidnappers. The sniper attempt ends with 2 kidnappers dead, and the remaining 7 terrorists and 9 hostages aboard the pilotless helicopters. An hour-long stalemate ensues, and just past midnight the terrorists open fire on the hostages with an AK-47, then explode a grenade inside the cockpit. The long ordeal ends with 11 hostages dead, 5 terrorists dead and 3 in custody.

Control and balance make it a beautiful experience.

Most people look at waves and just see water. To them, a road's just pavement. But if you think there's more to life, we've got something for you.

Mustang's new Sprint Decor Option. Sporty colors, inside and out. Dual racing mirrors that look right at home.

Even the interior of the Sprint Decor Option is a new experience. A panoramic instrument panel and a floor-mounted stick shift sitting between bucket seats. Now this is the real way to control a car.

Its stabilizer bar and independent front suspension help give you a more balanced ride. Around curves and over bumps.

The Sprint Decor Option is available in the Hardtop and SportsRoof models. Mag wheels, raised white letter tires and competition suspension are also available.

1972 Ford Mustang SportsRoof shown with Sprint Decor Option.

FORD MUSTANG

FORD DIVISION *Ford*

1972 Ford Mustang Hardtop shown with Sprint Decor Option.

Say What???

Comedian **George Carlin** is arrested on obscenity charges after performing his now infamous "Seven Words You Can Never Say on Television" at Summerfest, an annual music festival held in Milwaukee, Wisconsin. The case against Carlin is eventually dismissed.

The War is Over!

A World War II Japanese sergeant, **Shōichi Yokoi**, is found in the jungles of Guam where he has been hiding in a cave for the past 28 years. He was afraid to come out of hiding even after finding flyers stating the war had ended. Upon his return to Japan he is quoted as saying, "It is with much embarrassment that I have returned alive."

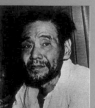

Saying Goodbye

Former U.S. President **Harry S. Truman** dies the day after Christmas at the age of 88 in Kansas City.

One for the Record Books

Yugoslavian stewardess **Vesna Vulović** survives falling 33,330' when the airplane she is on explodes over Czechoslovakia. She is the only survivor, and the accident earns her a place in the Guinness Book of World Records for surviving the highest fall without a parachute.

Lies, Lies, Lies

Author **Clifford Irving** claims to have collaborated with **Howard Hughes** on an autobiography of the reclusive, eccentric billionaire. Hughes eventually exposes the claim as a hoax and Irving is later convicted of fraud, spending 17 months in prison.

This 'n' That

Beetle vs. Model T

The Ford Model T can no longer claim the highest sales of any vehicle when Volkswagen sells their 15,007,034th Beetle.

The population of Yugoslavia has been vaccinated against smallpox for the past 50 years. The disease is considered eradicated after the last case in 1930, so when a man returns from a pilgrimage to Mecca with the disease, doctors are slow to recognize the symptoms. Once they realize what they are dealing with, the government reacts swiftly, closing borders, declaring martial law and setting up blockades. The efforts pay off and just 175 cases and 35 deaths are reported.

On Stone Mountain in Georgia the world's largest bas-relief sculpture is completed on March 3rd. The granite mountain boasts a huge, three-acre carving depicting three Confederate Civil War leaders, President Jefferson Davis, General Robert E. Lee and General "Stonewall" Jackson upon their favorite steeds, Blackjack, Traveller and Old Sorrel. The carving was conceived by Mrs. C. Helen Plane way back in 1912 and had been worked on intermittently since it was started in 1916.

Motor Trend Magazine has named the '72 Rally Nova "Compact Car of the Year."

Maybe it was the stripes?

It takes more than style and stripes to win a *Motor Trend* award.

Did you know, for example, that the *Motor Trend* staff tested over 100 cars from all over the world before finally selecting this year's seven winners?

Tested them thoroughly. Compared performance, features, strengths, weaknesses. Took a close look at workmanship. Dug deep. Discussed. Then voted.

We're delighted that our Rally Nova was a winner.

Motor Trend calls it "the happy culmination of what's happened with the Nova in the past seven years."

True.

And we appreciate the kind words.

But at the same time, you can be sure we're going to keep finding ways to make Nova an even better car.

Because we want your new Nova to be the best car you ever owned.

Stripes and all.

Rally Nova and friends beside the Hudson River at Cold Spring, N.Y.

Highway safety begins at home. Buckle up before you leave.

Chevrolet. Building a better way to see the U.S.A.

Apollo 16 blasts off on April 16th and returns on the 27th. It is the tenth manned mission, the fifth mission to land on the Moon, and the first to land in the Descartes highland region. The crew consists of John W. Young, T. Kenneth Mattingly Jr. and Charles M. Duke Jr. A relatively minor problem delays the lunar landing, and also shortens the mission by a day. The astronauts discover that areas previously considered to have been volcanic activity, are actually rocks formed by meteorite impacts, and in performance tests on the Lunar Rover it reaches a top speed of 11 mph, which is still the record.

Apollo 17 leaves Earth on December 7th, returning on December 19th; it's the sixth and final lunar landing mission. The crew consists of Eugene A. Cernan, Ronald E. Evans and Harrison H. Schmitt. Cernan and Schmitt explore the lunar surface while Evans orbits above. The mission returns the largest amount of lunar samples to date, and sets records for the longest manned lunar landing flight, longest total time spent in lunar surface extravehicular activities, and longest time in lunar orbit. The famous picture of Earth, known as "The Blue Marble" (below right), is taken on the mission. Cernan is the last person to walk on the Moon's surface and leaves with these words: "...We leave as we came and, God willing, as we shall return, with peace and hope for all mankind. Godspeed the crew of *Apollo 17*."

Here Man completed his first explorations of the moon. December 1972 AD. May the spirit of peace in which we came be reflected in the lives of all mankind.

Words from the plaque left on the Moon commemorating man's achievement in space exploration.

Some Firsts From 1972

* Atari is founded by Nolan Bushnell and Ted Dabney this year. In November Atari introduces the world to the arcade game Pong, paving the way for the future of video games.

* The FBI begins hiring women agents for the first time.

* *Deep Throat*, one of the first porn films with a plot line and character development, is released this year, garnering mainstream attention and starting a trend of "porn chic."

* On the CBS television show *Maude*, viewers and advertisers are shocked when Bea Arthur's character decides to go through with an abortion.

* Home Box Office (HBO), the nation's first pay-TV network, is launched by Charles Dolan and Gerald Levin of Sterling Manhattan Cable.

* Rose Heilbron becomes the first woman judge at the Old Bailey in London.

* The Magnavox Odyssey, the world's first home video game, hits stores in August. Sales flounder due to poor advertising and consumers thinking it could only be used with Magnavox TVs. Atari's home video game, Pong, will sweep the market in three years.

* The world's first pocket calculator with trigonometric and exponential functions, the HP-5 by Hewlett-Packard, is introduced and retails for $395.

* Wham-O introduces Silly String, colored plastic string shot as a fast-drying liquid from an aerosol can.

Corvette.
Everything you need is standard except the gas.

In 1953, we set out to build an American sports car because there wasn't one. Little did we know that 19 years later it would still be the only production sports car made in this country.

That's our Corvette. A classic. A legend. A car with as good a reputation as any car in the world.

Like all great cars, Corvette's price might make you stretch your budget a little. But like all great cars, you get a lot for your money. We think you get the *most* for your money in Corvette.

The list of standard equipment is impressive and extensive. A 4-Speed fully synchronized transmission. A 350-cubic-inch V8 with a 4-barrel carb. Disc brakes at all four wheels. Fully independent suspension all the way around. Positraction rear axle.

Full instrumentation including tach, ammeter, oil pressure gauge and temperature gauge.

The list goes on through carpeting, hidden windshield wipers, pop-up headlights and Astro Ventilation.

The point is that Corvette's standards aren't bare necessities. Along with all the excitement, they're the things most people want in a sports car. You might like to order air conditioning, an AM/FM/Stereo radio, leather seats, and a few other extras, but there just aren't too many things you can add to Corvette. When you buy a Corvette, about everything you need is standard . . . except the gas. And even that is no lead, low lead or regular.

Corvette Convertible with extra-cost hardtop at Great Smoky Mountains National Park.

There's so much to see, make sure you're around to see it. Buckle up.

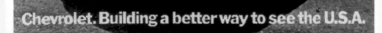

Chevrolet. Building a better way to see the U.S.A.

Huffy bikes
are geared for your pleasure.

The Tourister 5 · 5 Speeds · Twist Grip shift control

The Olympia Deluxe 10 · 10 Speeds · 27´ wheels

You're in for a pleasant surprise when you get out on a Huffy bike.

Because Huffy bikes are geared for fun. Whether you're on a 5 or 10 speed derailleur model or one of our 3 speed lightweights.

Each one has high-speed gears for level stretches. Powerful low gears to make molehills out of mountains. In-between gears to let you take in scenery and sounds at your own pace.

So get on the Huffy bike geared to your style.

And find yourself some fun.

Huffman, Dayton, Ohio 45401 or Azusa, California 91702.

Everyone deserves a Huffy. At least once in his life.

1972 Advertisements

NOW! YOU CAN JOIN THE DAVID CASSIDY FAN CLUB!

the very first club that's all DAVID and the only official DAVID CASSIDY FAN CLUB!

Vibra~Bra ™
the bra that helps make it possible to go without one!

MONSTER

7 FEET TALL IN AUTHENTIC COLORS

GLOW in the DARK EYES

ONLY $1.00

BOYS can Now Learn by Mail to Mount Birds and Animals

TRY THESE WIGS FREE FOR 30 DAYS!

...and if you are not COMPLETELY SATISFIED with the way these 1805 Kanekalon Wigs look, wear and feel, just return your wig and your purchase price will be refunded in full.

Now that your hair is longer, you need Wella Balsam.

SCIENCE

President Nixon orders NASA to begin a space shuttle program.

The dust storms that have been hiding the surface of Mars from *Mariner 9* since it started orbiting the planet last November finally settle, and *Mariner 9* is able to send the first clear pictures of the planet's surface back to Earth.

One of the largest solar flares ever recorded knocks out cable lines in the U.S. in early August.

A dramatic change in the field of biological science begins when the concept of recombinant DNA is published late in the year.

The Soviet's *Luna 20* reaches the surface of the Moon in February, and the unmanned mission returns samples from the surface that are shared with American and French scientists.

Pioneer 10, the first man-made satellite to leave our solar system, is launched from Cape Kennedy.

Earth Resources Technology Satellite 1, later renamed *Landsat 1*, is launched from Vandenberg Air Force Base in California this July. It is the first satellite that serves the purpose of acquiring imagery of Earth from space.

Nobel Prizes

PHYSICS
"for their jointly developed theory of superconductivity, usually called the BCS-theory"

**John Bardeen
Leon Neil Cooper
John Robert Schrieffer**

CHEMISTRY
"for his work on ribonuclease..."

Christian B. Anfinsen

"... connection between chemical structure and catalytic activity of the active centre of the ribonuclease molecule"

**Stanford Moore
William H. Stein**

PHYSIOLOGY OR MEDICINE

"for their discoveries concerning the chemical structure of antibodies"

**Gerald M. Edelman
Rodney R. Porter**

BORN IN 1972

JOHNSON

AFFLECK

Ben Affleck

Cameron Diaz

Carmen Electra

Eminem

Jennifer Garner

Geri Halliwell

Mia Hamm

Dwayne Johnson

Jude Law

Jenny McCarthy

Alyssa Milano

Gretchen Mol

Shaquille O'Neal

Brad Paisley

Gwyneth Paltrow

Amanda Peet

Busta Rhymes

Rebecca Romijn

Gabrielle Union

LAW

ELECTRA

McCARTHY

HALLIWELL

PAISLEY

HAMM

PALTROW

Fashion 1972

What you're looking for now: A classic way to kick off the season.

It's time to pick out your this-year's wardrobe. And this outfit belongs in it.

Fresh. Crisp. It can follow you anywhere.

Start with a white stock tie blouse that's machine washable. Add a great tartan pant. 100% polyester that's also machine washable. And, layered over it all, the classic black blazer of woven acrylic.

This kind of outfit's always right. And the price is right, too.

Look for it in the misses' sportswear department at most Sears, Roebuck and Co. larger stores. Or look for it in the catalog. Or call Catalog Shopping Service.

For a beautiful, wearable wardrobe.

Stylin' Shoes

For Him

For Her

WINTER OLYMPICS

The Winter Olympics in Sapporo, Hokkaido, Japan, are the first games to be held outside of either Europe or North America.

Never having won a gold medal in the Winter Olympics, Japan sweeps the 70m ski jump, winning gold, silver, and bronze.

Three days before the games the IOC president threatens to disqualify 40 skiers for receiving endorsements and other deals. Canada refuses to send an ice hockey team, stating that there are no restrictions on pros from communist nations.

These are the last games where a gold medal was won by a skier on wooden skis.

WINTER MEDAL COUNT

GOLD MEDALS	
USSR	8
East Germany	4
Switzerland	4
Netherlands	4
USA	3

TOTAL MEDALS	
USSR	16
East Germany	14
Norway	12
Switzerland	10
Netherlands	9

SUMMER MEDAL COUNT

GOLD MEDALS	
USSR	50
USA	33
East Germany	20
West Germany	13

TOTAL MEDALS	
USSR	99
USA	94
East Germany	
West Germany	

SUMMER OLYMPICS

The Summer Olympics take place in Munich, Germany. They are only the second Summer Olympics to be held in Germany. The games' official motto is "The Happy Games."

American swimmer **Mark Spitz** sets a world record with 7 gold medals at a single Olympics, and sets a new world record in each of those events.

Australian swimmer **Shane Gould** wins 3 gold medals, 1 silver, and 1 bronze at the age of 15.

Called "the most controversial game in international basketball history," the **Soviets** defeat the **U.S.** 51-50. The U.S. does not accept its silver medal.

A diminutive 17-year-old gymnast, **Olga Korbut**, captivates audiences and captures hearts across the globe with her acrobatic routines and genuine displays of emotion. Born in the Russian Republic of Belarus, Korbut is a member of the Soviet team. She quickly becomes a media favorite, winning 3 gold medals and 1 silver, and the title of "Athlete of the Year" from ABC's *Wide World of Sports*.

Archery and handball matches are held at the games for the first time since 1920 and 1936 respectivley, and slalom canoeing is held for the first time.

FOOTBALL

PRO BALL

The inbound lines are moved closer to the field center. At 18'6" apart they are now the same width as the goalposts. Also new this year is tie games will now be counted in winning percentages as a half-game win and a half-game loss.

The Divisional Playoffs at the end of the season see the **Miami Dolphins** over **Cleveland Browns** 20-14: **Pittsburgh Steelers** over **Oakland Raiders** 13-7; **Dallas Cowboys** over **San Francisco 49ers** 30-28; and **Washington Redskins** over **Green Bay Packers** 16-3. The **Dolphins** take the **Steelers** 21-17 and the **Redskins** beat the **Cowboys** 26-3 for the Conference Championships. The final showdown of the 1972 NFL season is played at **Super Bowl VII** in January 1973 at Los Angeles Coliseum. The unstoppable AFC **Dolphins** beat the NFC **Redskins** 14-7, making them the first team ever to have an undefeated and untied championship season!

COLLEGE BALL

Coach **John McKay** leads the **USC Trojans** in an undefeated season, winning the National Championship.

Orange Bowl
Nebraska
over **Notre Dame**
40-6

Cotton Bowl
Texas
over **Alabama**
17-13

Sugar Bowl
Oklahoma
over **Penn State**
14-0

Rose Bowl
USC
over **Ohio State**
42-17

Heisman Trophy
Johnny Rodgers
Nebraska

Vince Lombardi Award
Rich Glover
Nebraska

A players' strike cancels the first two weeks of the season.

WORLD SERIES

Oakland Athletics

over

Cincinnati Reds 4-3

The Athletics return to the World Series after 41 years lead by Series MVP Gene Tenace with four homers, two on his first two at bats.

A plane crash on New Year's Eve claims the life of Pittsburgh Pirate right fielder **Roberto Clemente.** His last hit was the fabled 3,000th of his career.

Most Valuable Player
Dick Allen (AL)
Johnny Bench (NL)

Cy Young Award
Gaylord Perry (AL)
Steve Carlton (NL)

Rookie of the Year
Carlton Fisk (AL)
Jon Matlack (NL)

Clemente

Bench

WORLD SERIES 72

PIRATES 21

BASEBALL

HOCKEY

Going into the semifinals this season, the Boston Bruins face off against the St. Louis Blues, whom they trounce 4-0, while the New York Rangers are busy crushing the Chicago Blackhawks 4-0. The Bruins defeat the Rangers 4-2 and take home the Stanley Cup.

Prince of Wales Trophy
Boston Bruins

Art Ross Trophy
Phil Esposito
Boston Bruins

Bill Masterton Memorial Trophy
Bobby Clarke
Philadelphia Flyers

Calder Memorial Trophy
Ken Dryden
Montreal Canadiens

Hart Memorial Trophy
Bobby Orr
Boston Bruins

Lady Byng Memorial Trophy
Jean Ratelle
New York Rangers

Vezina Trophy
Tony Esposito & **Gary Smith**
Chicago Blackhawks

PRO BALL

The Western Conference semifinals see the **L.A. Lakers** face the **Chicago Bulls** and win 4-0, and the **Milwaukee Bucks** defeat the **Golden State Warriors** 4-1. Meanwhile in the Eastern Conference the **Boston Celtics** beat the **Atlanta Hawks** 4-2, while the **New York Knicks** defeat the **Baltimore Bullets** 4-2. In the Conference finals the **Lakers** take the **Bucks** 4-2 and the **Knicks** beat the **Celtics** 4-1. The **Lakers** take the Championship from the **Knicks** 4-1.

COLLEGE BALL

In the Final Four **Florida State** beats **North Carolina** 79-75 and **UCLA** beats **Louisville** 96-77. For their eighth NCAA Championship, coach **John Wooden** leads **UCLA** to a victory over **Florida State**, 81-76. UCLA's **Bill Walton** wins the Naismith College Player of the Year award.

BASKETBALL